Tombstone Lettering

in the British Isles / Alan Bartram

Lund Humphries, London / Watson-Guptill Publications, New York

First edition 1978
Published by
Lund Humphries Publishers Ltd
26 Litchfield Street London WC2

SBN 85331 414 4

First published 1978 in the United States
by Watson-Guptill Publications
a division of Billboard Publications, Inc.
1515 Broadway, New York, N.Y. 10036

ISBN 0–8230–5380–6

Library of Congress Catalog Card Number 78–52350

Designed by Alan Bartram
Made and printed in Great Britain
by W & J Mackay Ltd, Chatham, Kent

Tombstone Lettering

This is not a book about epitaphs, or messages on tombstones, or unusual and eccentric tombstones. Nor is it intended to be a fully comprehensive history of the subject, for certain regions are very thinly covered, if at all. This is a book of lettering, more specifically lettering chosen to show the breadth and general sequence of the English lettering tradition. I have chosen tombstones to illustrate this because I believe this field shows the subject at its purest. The letters are entirely the creation of lettercutters, undictated-to by architects, designers, printers, and so on. The carvers are simply following their tradition, their instincts, their preferences, and the discipline of their craft; though they always have an eye in the back of their heads, noting what is going on in other fields. The work of the writing masters, for instance, had a particularly decisive influence on them.

That said, I hope the reader will also enjoy the messages on the stones, or the incidental designs around the lettering, or the overall design. But the selection has been made primarily on the letterform.

Nothing is as simple as it seems, and the idea that one might just arrange the tombstones in chronological order, as revealed by the carved dates, and leave them to tell the story on their own, does not of course work out in practice. Many geographical and local influences disturb this pleasing notion: fashions took longer to reach some places than others; some cutters were more adventurous, some more traditional, than others; local customs had their effect; the local stone had *its* effect. And anyway one cannot always tell from the date when the stone was cut, for often one stone will commemorate a whole family, after a particularly successful, or proud, member of the family had decided that all members for several generations should be commemorated by a really showy affair truly worthy of them, regardless of where they are buried, perhaps replacing the more humble, earlier, individual stones. Even then, later generations may add their names to it, and some stones are themselves a short history of lettering styles, the forms getting, usually, less skilled as they get nearer to our time.

Moreover, lettering is a living tradition, and cannot be bundled into boxes marked with style and date. The shuffling around into classifications is a fairly recent game of the last forty or fifty years, and lettering historians, typographers and lettering artists are still arguing, often rather heatedly, about the respective merits of one system of classification as opposed to another. I have ignored most of this, and tried to show the route of general developments, giving a few basic signposts on the way.

Few headstones appear to have survived from before about 1600 (a date which also seems to mark the beginning of carved lettering on buildings in this country). It seems likely, however, that wooden monuments preceded those of stone, and the earlier forms of stone-carved letters sometimes reflect this. The carving of letters in relief, in stone an extremely laborious technique, seems to be an example of tradition overcoming expedience. The forms were very primitive, just as in such architectural lettering as has survived. They consisted of either rather heavy letters (usually capitals), their strokes of more or less even weight with triangular terminations (too blunt to be dignified by the term serif); or similar letters without these terminations – what we would now call sans serifs. Often a few lower-case letters were scattered among the capitals. Somewhat later, the forms became a little more regular (they could hardly have become less so), and rather truer serifs began to emerge, possibly as the natural consequence of a desire for a neat termination to the strokes. The proportions of the letters cannot be called truly roman, and I prefer to lump all these forms, seriffed (true or in embryo), and non-seriffed, under the term primitive.

Many of the earlier stones I show come from the Vale of Belvoir, and in this area the use of slate, a beautiful stone for cutting letters, has its effect on the letterform. Soft enough for cutting without undue labour, fine enough to allow the delicate flourishes which appeared later, with little tendency to flake, and durable, it has allowed lettercutters the opportunity to develop their craft and their forms. Those here show characteristics which were to become increasingly marked, though refined, in English lettering generally. The earlier examples are clumsy and heavy, but even they have the undeniable vigour and, what shall we call it? – love? – enthusiasm? – high spirits? – which has been such a potent element throughout the story of English lettering. There is no need for all those flourishes and spirals, except the need of the cutter to show off, or express his pleasure and pride in his work. Without being clever or paradoxical, one has to say these headstones show immense *joie-de-vivre*, far more than any Roman lettercutters showed in their varied, subtle and sensitive forms. One is reminded that fantasy and invention were also characteristic of the work done in the Celtic monasteries.

The enthusiasm and need for expression was the force which, charging the realisation that letters had great inherent possibilities for formal invention, created the English vernacular tradition. More specifically, it was the force which created what I have called the english letter, a major and still vital contribution to letterforms. It differs from what is thought of as the 'normal' roman, a form given definitive shape in print by the great Venetian, French, and Dutch printers, by somewhat different proportions of the letters relative to one another, and, originally, heaviness and clumsiness of form. This later became greatly refined, and grew into a letter which, compared to the 'normal' roman such as Bembo, in which this book is set, usually has bolder thick strokes, finer thin strokes, and a fairly abrupt transition from thicks to thins. Its stress, that is the angle of the thick stroke in a curved form such as the O or G, is vertical, not at the slight angle of a roman; the serifs are horizontal (thus correctly at right angles to the stress) and are rich and pointed. Capital letters are the same height as the ascenders of lower-case letters (whereas in printers' roman old face letters, the capitals are slightly smaller). Within these limits – artificial limits, created for tidy-minded pigeon-holers – can be found a fine variety of subtle forms. In print, John Baskerville was the first to create the form, in 1754, although the French Roman du Roi of 1702 had some of these characteristics. Its gestation was gradual and long-drawn out, and occurred in many areas simultaneously; once born, however, it grew apace.

Many examples shown here, from the earliest onwards, have swirls and flourishes of all kinds; but these are not an intrinsic part of the form, merely an embellishment made as a whim of the carver. These flourishes later became an important part of the overall design of the headstones. The earlier examples appear to have been the result of the carver's reaction to the seductive nature of the slate; but the later examples clearly show the influence of the writing masters of the first half of the eighteenth century: their copy books were frequently used as patterns by the lettercutters. Similar though less elaborate flourishes can be seen on headstones from northern England, where the stone is harder and less amenable to such *tours-de-force*.

As part of this development, the use of scripts, in which letters are linked up in a continuous flowing line, became more widespread, together with their related form, the italic. This latter is basically a script where the individual letters stay separate, although it developed certain other characteristics of its own. Either form tended to result in the carver getting carried away, extending the letters into flourishes and swirls. The pressure strokes of the writing masters' pens, giving the elegant thick-and-thin forms, were faithfully imitated by the carvers (the thick strokes also biting deeper into the stone). So at this period, alongside forms which grew out of the stone-carving tradition itself, there developed a variety of styles lifted straight out of the calligraphers' copy books. The two streams often

The deaths in one family over eighty years. A stone at Great Crosthwaite, Cumberland (**1**). The last four lines were added after the stone had been put up; hence their slant. Such stones can show greater variation of styles than this, as entries are added from generation to generation; and, often confusingly, unlike here, no date of erection is given.

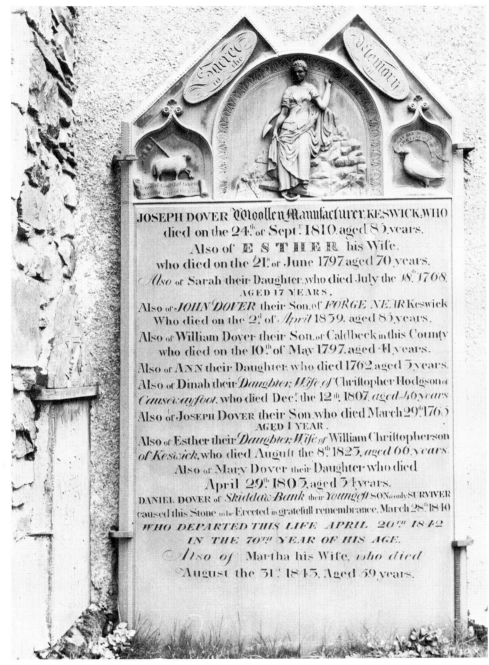

1

mingled on the same stone; and even today faint echoes of the calligraphers' flourishes swirl around a few letters, when all other signs of this influence have disappeared.

A form which appears in these pictures as a development of the english letter is one where the shading, or transition from thick strokes to thin, becomes even more abrupt, and the serifs become merely a horizontal hair line. A typographer would term this form a modern and it developed from French models. It is not always easy to draw the dividing line between an english letter and a modern.

The influence of the writing masters' copy books was at this time also responsible for many decorative letterforms. The gothic letter appeared in variety, from a quite delicate, almost romanised, style to a heavy angular form. Sometimes, by using only the capital letters, and adding numerous flourishes, total illegibility was achieved. Some of the simpler and bolder forms were well suited to the harder stones of the north of England. Other decorative letters of this period were achieved by carving patterns (dots, diamonds, stripes, flowers, leaves, and so on) within the strokes of the letters, although the form itself was still the traditional english letter.

Whilst the use of slate in the Vale of Belvoir encouraged decorative letters, extended flourishes, and elements of non-lettering decoration, resulting in highly rococo headstones, extremely decorative effects were also achieved by more austere combinations, which harder northern stones made inevitable. These effects were obtained by subtle oppositions of upright lower case, italic lower case, lines or words in capitals or italic capitals, with the occasional script, rarer gothic letter, and sparsely used flourish. The first word of the inscription was often isolated to allow elaborately decorative treatment. Many small devices were employed to enliven the overall pattern. These developments occurred at a somewhat later date than the rococo Belvoir examples – early nineteenth century, rather than late eighteenth. More austere they may have been, but there is nothing dour about them. Their 'masculinity' makes an interesting contrast with the more 'feminine' Belvoir stones, and one feels an affinity between them and the vigour and forthrightness of the Victorian engineers.

So far, I have only discussed the decorative forms restricted to embellishments on traditional letterforms. However, the early nineteenth century saw a new development, brought about in printing by the demands of trade and advertising, and in architecture by romantic ideas of antiquity and 'correct' form for classical buildings. These new requirements resulted in a sudden burst of invention by letter designers, the effect of which permeated far beyond their origins. Tombstone cutters were not immune, those in Cornwall being particularly influenced.

The early history of these new English forms is still not too clear, and exactly how they originated is not known. The development of all letter forms is a slow and continuing process, a gradual synthesising of a preference which is in the air for a certain kind of form. These new Victorian forms probably first made their appearance on buildings, but were soon shown in typefounders' specimen books.

The form known as clarendon is essentially a bold version of the english letter. With bold thick strokes, somewhat less bold thins, and bracketed square-cut serifs (that is, having square outer ends, but flowing, curving, into the stroke), they can be found in a wide variety of weights and widths, and in rich forms with a marked difference between thicks and thins, or more austere versions with little difference.

When a somewhat similar letter is given slab serifs – that is, square ends and no bracketing to the junction of serif and stroke – it is called (for no good reason) an egyptian. This too is a very versatile form.

If a rather similar letter has no serifs, it is called a grotesque. The strokes of this letter can be of even weight, but usually, especially in bolder forms, there is some, perhaps much, variation in the weights of thicks and thins. Again, this is a form with tremendous scope for variation within its basic character. A rather subtle sub-division of this form is the sans serif, whose proportions are generally derived from the classical romans, whereas clarendon, egyptians and grotesques have somewhat different basic proportions more in common with the english letter.

All these versions can be found in decorative forms, made by the addition of shadows or inlines of various kinds. Clarendons and egyptians are rarely italicised,

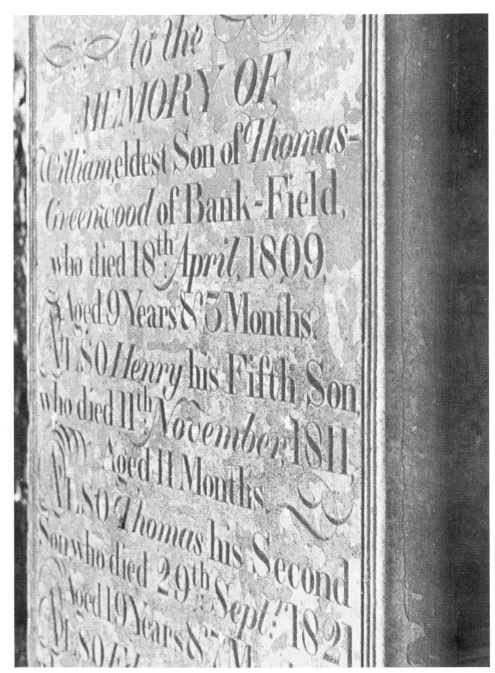

A lively texture could be achieved by simple means. From Halifax, Yorkshire, (**2**) has freely-used italics and swash capitals on a hard northern stone. This example also demonstrates the mainstream lettercarving style, more or less un-influenced by either the writing masters or by printers.

Two stones demonstrate the two major influences on lettercutters during the eighteenth and nineteenth centuries. At Loughborough, Leicestershire (3), the influence is that of the writing masters and their pattern books, as was general in the Midlands. The slightly later stone from Lostwithiel, Cornwall (4) was affected by the printing of the time, both in the letter-forms used and the way they were used, although a calligraphic influence is also present. This is an unusually good example of the preferred influence of the West Country cutters.

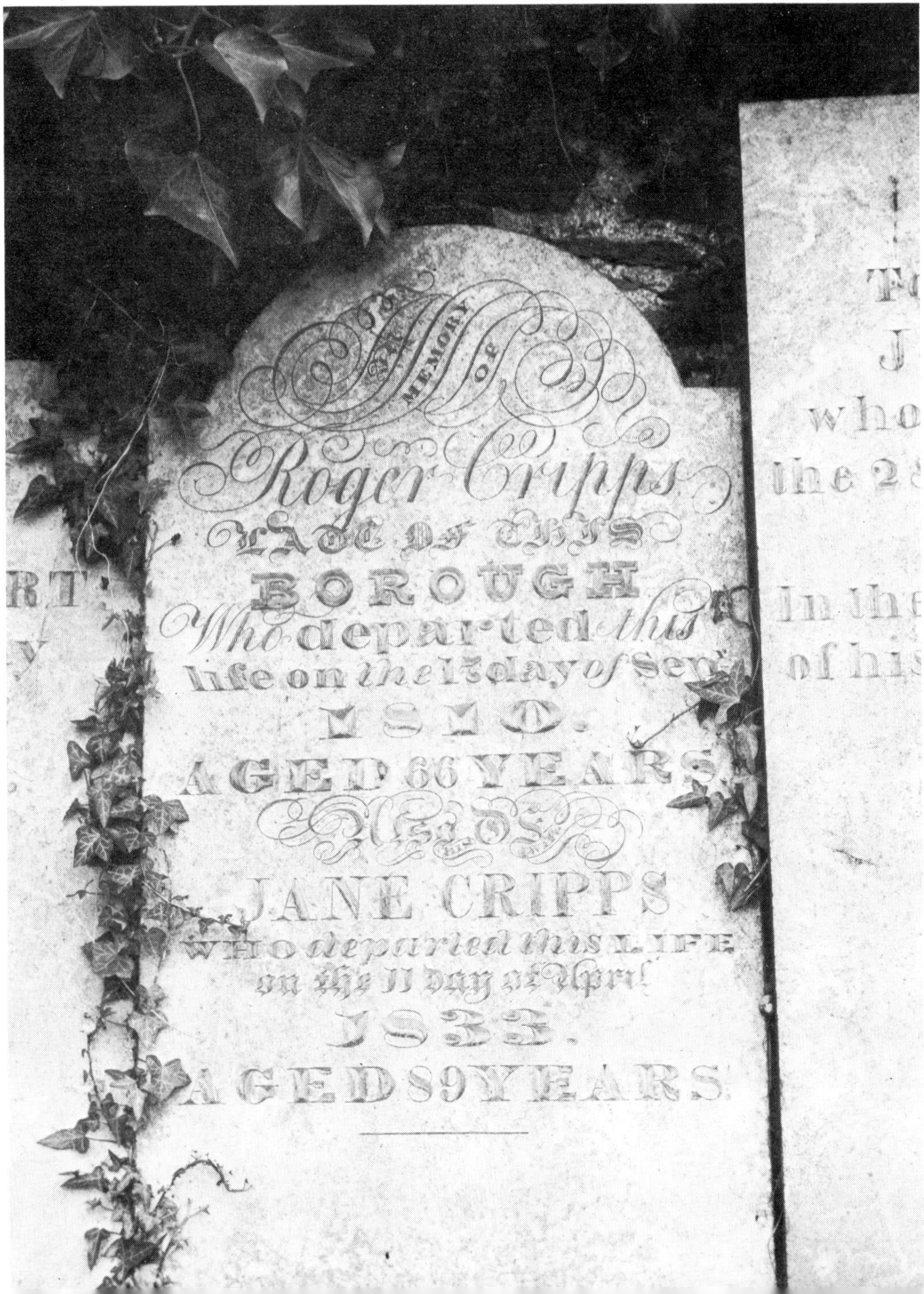

In
Memory
of
Roger Cripps
LATE OF THIS
BOROUGH
Who departed this
life on the 13 day of Sep.r
1810.
AGED 66 YEARS
Also of
JANE CRIPPS
WHO departed this LIFE
on the 11 day of April
1833.
AGED 89 YEARS

4

A proudly-signed stone from Hatherleigh, Devon (5).

but grotesques can often be seen in inclined versions.

My final classification is 'decorative'. The three former categories can be lavishly ornamented; but as well as such forms, new inventions became more and more prolific as the Victorians demanded more and more novelties. This period of imagination and originality has only been rivalled by that created today by filmsetting and dry transfer lettering.

It was some time before these fine new forms found much use outside the British Isles, and then, in Europe, it was for some time mainly the grotesque or, later, the more extreme decorative letters, which were taken up; clarendons and egyptians were rarely, perhaps never, used there for much except print. In America, however, all forms were quickly accepted and used with enthusiasm, skill, and invention. Delight in the possibilities of lettering forms has been as great there, if not even greater, than in Britain.

The later history of headstones is rather depressing. The heights were reached in the first half of the nineteenth century, or perhaps earlier. Thereafter the decline is steady until we reach the dregs of today. All love and enthusiasm left the craft. A few of the old tricks survived as conventions for giving some superficial elegance to the design. Nothing new, absolutely nothing, was thought up. Harder and harder, deader and deader, the fine virile tradition degenerated into just another job to be done as quickly and cheaply as possible. If it wasn't cheap, it was tasteless. At its peak, the carver was proud to sign his work – sometimes his name is almost as prominent as the person the stone commemorates. Whole families of lettercutters can be traced on the stones of Belvoir. But today the joy of lettering, the pleasure in guiding the chisel through a fine material, is nowhere apparent. Nor is any interest apparent in what is happening to lettering elsewhere. Eyes seem only turned towards the past, if they are turned anywhere.

I hope and imagine there are exceptions to this depressing situation. I have only seen one group myself, at Carbury in the Irish Republic. Tasteful adaptations of old forms are carved by a few survivors of the Arts and Crafts Movement – a cut above the old tradesmen – but these usually show little innovating spirit, merely a nostalgia for the Good Old Days. Nowhere is there any awareness that type designs, and the positioning of type on a page, has undergone any change in the last fifty years.

Parallel to the increasing mechanisation of life is a reaction against it. The craft of thatching, for instance, has undergone quite a revival, as have numerous other crafts. Not only is there a demand for them, there are also young people eager to be trained for them. Perhaps something similar will happen to letter carving. It has a similar appeal as carpentry – working with beautiful natural materials which demand understanding and skill to exploit their latent possibilities. Its scope for self-expression is boundless. The translation, into terms of stone, of contemporary developments in lettering and design, is a demanding challenge in almost virgin territory. The major obstacle is probably economic – as in so many worthwhile things. But the craft was well into its decline before economic factors could have affected it, so probably the climate of opinion is of equal importance. It may be that this climate is improving. In many fields, the craft of lettering is still alive, if not always vigorous. If a need or a demand is strong enough, means to meet the need will often grow of their own. I think the interest in good lettering is no less than it was, say, fifty years ago; and taste is probably higher. The question remains, how many people wish to be commemorated by a highly durable piece of carved stone, rather than by perhaps the planting of a tree, or nothing at all?

MICHAEL HENCHARD'S WILL
From Thomas Hardy's *The Mayor of Casterbridge*.

That Elizabeth-Jane Farfrae be not told of my death,
or made to grieve on account of me.
& that I be not bury'd in consecrated ground.
& that no sexton be asked to toll the bell.
& that nobody is wished to see my dead body.
& that no murners walk behind me at my funeral.
& that no flours be planted on my grave.
& that no man remember me.
To this I put my name.   Michael Henchard

A sequence of twelve pictures (6–17) attempts to show briefly the development of English letterforms, illustrating points made in the introduction and summarising the progression depicted by this book.

Primitive: *From Colne, Lancashire, (6) shows a chunky sans serif form of more or less even weight. The As have a top cross-bar typical of the period, and the strokes swell a little at their ends. (7) from Langar, Nottinghamshire, has incipient serifs, and strokes changing from thick to thin; but it cannot be called a roman letter. The thicker, stressed, parts of circular letters are on a vertical axis – like the english letter which developed from this form.*

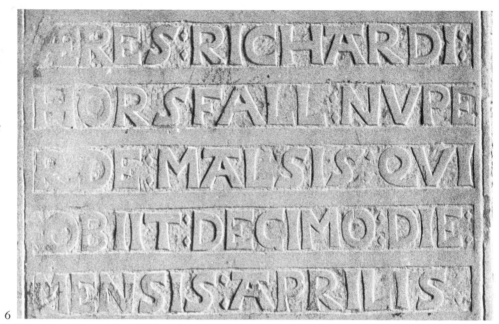

6

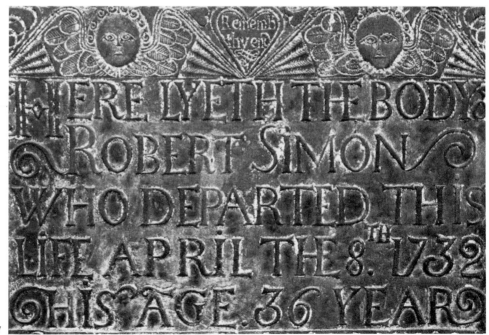

7

English: *Two examples show early stages of development: (8) from Thorne, Yorkshire, (9) from Lostwithiel, Cornwall. All the basic characteristics are seen in both: a marked difference between thick and thin strokes, the one flowing quickly into the other; a vertical stress; stems flowing into serifs, although in (8) these are uncharacteristically slanting instead of the horizontal ones seen in (9) which became usual; and a round, generous form. The decorative letters are still fundamentally the same form, except for the 'Here' of (9), in calligraphic black or gothic letter.*

8

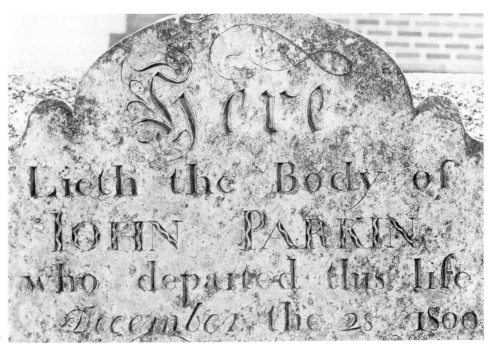

9

English: *The Halifax, Yorkshire, stone* (**10**) *shows this letter in a definitive form. A more assured version of* (**9**), *its italic is also more worked out, with its looped serifs and occasional flourish. The word 'Memory' is in a skilful calligraphic gothic letter.*

Modern: *This stone from Grantham, Lincolnshire* (**11**) *shows the close relationship of the modern to the english letter. Typeforms reveal the difference more clearly. The shading-off from thick strokes to thin, and to serifs, is more abrupt (some moderns have none of this shading at all, the serifs being merely a horizontal hairline at the end of the stroke). It is a drier, more wiry form, relieved here by the exuberant flourishes. It is not necessarily lighter in weight than the english letter, though it is here.*

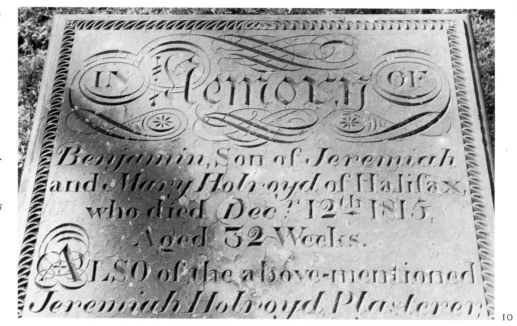

10

11

Clarendon: *Beneath an almost entirely illegible gothic letter, the 'In Memory' of (*12*) from Barnard Castle, Durham, is in two weights of clarendon. Essentially a bold english letter, the serifs are well-bracketed (curved at their junctions with the stroke) but with square-cut ends.*

Egyptian: *Also from Barnard Castle, (*13*) shows in 'HB' a normal form of this letter, with its unbracketed slab serifs; 'Sacred' is in a bolder, richer, variant.*

12

13

Grotesque: *From Burnley, Lancashire,* (**14**) *shows a grotesque in the words 'Memory' and 'Also'. These could be described as egyptians (such as seen in the word 'Pendle') without serifs. Like them, they are usually of fairly even weight and rather bold, and can be a very noble letter; but they rarely appear at their best on tombstones.* (**15**) *from Great Crosthwaite, Cumberland, shows a debased grotesque in the second, third, and sixth lines. The rest is a debased english letter, becoming a clarendon in places. This stone is a typical example of the stilted, unjoyous cutting of later lettering. Vestigial flourishes around the italic fail to enliven it.*

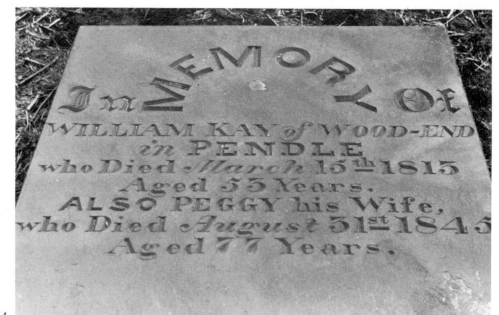

14

15

Decorative: *An endless variety of decorative letters appeared in the nineteenth century.* (**16**) *from St Minver, Cornwall, is a shadowed letter – commonly found in the West Country, and in print – a bold modern, often known as a fat face, given an illusion of three dimensions. Many such enrichments of normal letters were made.* (**17**) *from Wymondham, Leicestershire, has two kinds of decorated english letters in the words 'The' and 'Needham'. More different are the words 'of Henry and Jane' where the form itself creates the decorative effect.*

16

17

In iron-founding localities, old cast-iron grave-slabs can often be seen. The availability of charcoal in Kent and Sussex enabled founding to flourish there; in Wadhurst church, Sussex, are a number of slabs dating from the early seventeenth century. This one (**18**) is in the graveyard.

Stone of course is more destructible than iron, so most slabs are at the mercy of time, decay, or pollution. One cannot feel we have missed much in the way of beautiful lettering if we have lost many slabs from before the eighteenth century. These two (**19**) are from the remotely-situated abbey of Corcomroe, Co. Clare. Many of the old stones had the background cut away, the letters appearing in relief.

Another early example can be seen at Colne, Lancashire (**20**). The stone between the lines has been left: cutting it away is laborious, and the ridges have a pleasing effect.

Although still primitive, a relief letter from Hickling, Nottinghamshire (**21**) is a great advance, and enters the realms of folk art. An example of stones found around the Vale of Belvoir, it shows real feeling for, and delight in, letterforms. Another world.

The next few pages illustrate the letter-forms developed on their slate tombstones by the Vale of Belvoir cutters around 1710 to 1740. At Granby, Nottinghamshire (22), as elsewhere, these forms are seen both in relief and incised. Although unsophisticated, flourishes and little tricks of all kinds are exploited. This enthusiasm was to be the cause of a lot of wonderful things.

Some of the early stones were tiny, such as (23) from Langar, Nottinghamshire – even allowing for the rising of the ground level as more bodies were added. From Hickling, Nottinghamshire, (24) is again in relief and incised: a plainer and slightly earlier version of (21).

23

24

In these three stones we can see the beginnings of the english letter. The earliest of this Belvoir group, dated 1710, (25) is from Grantham, Lincolnshire; (26) and (27) are from Granby. The decorative swirls, spirals and flourishes appeared early in the development.

25

26

Old stones are often pulled up for lack of room; a better excuse than the tidy-mindedness frequently the cause of destroyed churchyards. These piles are from Nether Broughton, Leicestershire, (**28**) and (**29**).

28

WILLIAM THE SON
OF JOHN & ELIZABE
WRIGHT DIED MAR
THE II 1722

Here lies y Body of
Rebecca wife of will:
Barnet who departed
this life Dec y 28 1728
Aged 62 years

Tho death has parted you
Our bodys to dust must tour
I hope y we shall meet again
You have no cause to mou

Showing some affinity with the Belvoir stones, a memorial inside Winchcombe church, Gloucestershire (30) makes effective use of the flourishes of swash letters. Without them, it would be rather ordinary. Somehow such flourishes seem to be a very English thing. But then good lettering is an English thing: the inherent limitations appear to stimulate the imagination.

The lettering on (31) at Beaminster, Dorset, is not especially
distinguished, being faintly classical with rustic touches. It
is earlier than any of the Belvoir stones; and is one of my
few examples not carved in slate or hard northern stone.
So much good lettering has crumbled beyond the possibilities of photography.

The next four illustrations, from Moffat, Dumfriesshire, show an interesting development from the naïve. Of the first pair, (32) is almost like a child's writing; (33), although a little earlier in date, is more developed, with small flourishes and a definite V-cut to the incisions.

This second pair from Moffat shows further improvement: (**34**) seems to take the form of the double f and echo it in other letters; while (**35**), with its strange suggestion of hell-fire around the base, has become a properly-formed, rhythmical italic. We are out of the primitive, here.

35

The almost even-weight lettering on an early stone from Kilfenora Abbey, Co. Clare (**36**) is of roman form. From Muckross Abbey, Co. Kerry, (**37**) is less classical, thick and thin strokes having a sharper contrast; it includes an unexpected and effectively proficient piece of italic. A less sophisticated stone from Muckross (**38**) has an unusual mixture of capitals and lower-case letters reminding one of half-uncials.

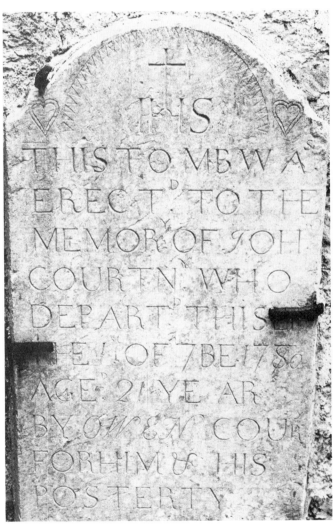

IHS

THIS TOMBE WA
ERECT^D TO THE
MEMOR OF IOH
COURTN WHO
DEPART^D THIS
EV^I OF 7BE 178o
AGE^D 21 YEAR
BY OWEN COUR
FOR HIM & HIS
POSTERTY

37

Here Lies
he body of
he rcuen Pa
RICK CONNO
no departed
his Life the 3o
OF decbr 178o
Iges 48 Yea

38

An early memorial in Bampton church, Oxfordshire (**39**) superficially looks later in feeling than anything yet, although it betrays its age in details like the 8. Simpler people employ simpler craftsmen; those with wealth or position reinforce it by using superior craftsmen. So we can get enormous disparities of style in any period.

From the North, (**40**) at Burnley, Lancashire, and (**41**) at Halifax, Yorkshire, show further development towards the english letter; (41) has a later addition actually in this form.

40

41

Near this Place lieth interred
the Body of Thomas Wren of Sea
toller in Borrowdale in the Parish
of Crosthwaite who departed this
Life the sixteenth day of February in
the year 1780 in the eighty fourth
year of his age.

HARK from the Tombs A dolefull Sound
Mine Ears attend the Cry
Ye Living men come view the ground
where you must shortly lie & c

More precursors of the english letter. (**42**) from Great Crosthwaite, Cumberland, has all its characteristics in essentials, but with a slight (and very pleasing) taste of the italic. (**43**) from nearby Cockermouth starts off with a more decidedly italic form, although very similar to the Crosthwaite example; it then becomes firmly upright, a true english letter; then – and this was clearly added later – it is the definitive form.

43

Three Irish stones using the english
letter in a personal way. (44) from
Carbury, Co. Kildare, has the rounded
feeling seen in (38) which is actually
chronologically later; whilst two from
Durrow, Co. Leix, (45) and (46), have
perhaps excessively emphasized
ascenders and descenders. Mr Martin
O'Connor was clearly proud of his
work, and rightly so.

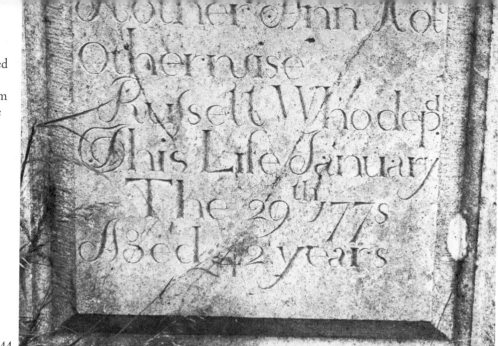

44

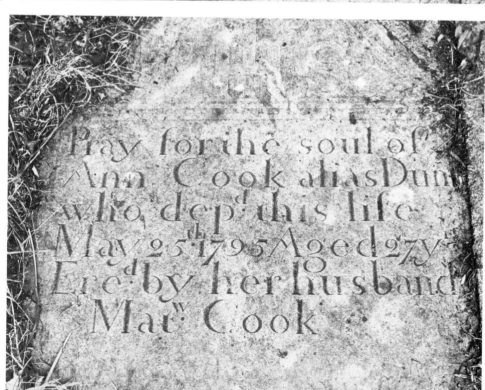

45

IHS

O God have Mercy on
the Soul of John Sulla
van who Dep.d Nov.r
the 29th 1786 aged 38 yrs
Er.d by his Brother
Thomas Sullavan
Martin O Connor Stonecutter
7 Curches

A final stone, for the time being, from the North, to show again the definitive english letter, boldly used at Barnard Castle, Durham (**47**). We now have to travel to the other end of the country to see what was happening there. Lettering being a living craft, it does not arrange itself for a tidy chronological progression; we shall be hopping around in time and space for a while yet.

I am very suspicious of the date on (47) – the letterform looks fifty years later. If it were the date of cutting, this stone from Holsworthy, Devon (48) is almost contemporary. The closely-packed text makes a pleasing pattern. In the West Country, the long pious verses frequently indulged in often necessitated smaller lettering.

This stone was actually lying on its side, which explains the otherwise oddly-behaved vegetation on the left.

Here
Lies the
body of Ber-
nard Weſtlake.
the Son of Hum
phrey Weſtlake.and
Eliz. his wife. who
Departed this Life
the 11. day of March.
1763. aged five years

Weep not for me my parents dear.
Lament me not nor ſhed a tear.
My joys are great with my redeemer fixed.
In heaven again I hope that we ſhall meet.
Where we with angels then that ſing.
The praiſes of our God and King.

This bold and rather clumsily-cut stone is from Lostwithiel, Cornwall (**49**). Less than ten years later, (**50**) from Chulmleigh, Devon, shows greater regularity and expertise, although the two pieces of lettering are not really so very different in essentials.

49

Here
lies the Body of John Faning
son of John & Elizabeth Faning
of this Town who departed
this life the 20th day of october
in the year of our Lord 1771
aged 3 years

Sweet babe of light, in Innocence aray'd
...w'n to this world, but for a better made
...d took him home, with him to sing
...lleluJah's to his Christ and King

50

I have already mentioned that a strictly chronological sequence will sometimes fall apart; this is one of those times, and for the next few pages I have tried to make a visual sequence. (**51**) from St Minver, Cornwall, for instance, is cruder than (**52**) from Bridestowe, Devon, cut thirty-seven years earlier in a sensitive and somewhat condensed variant of the english form. The cutter of the St Minver stone created such a contrast between thicks and thins, and such a sharp change between the two, that if it were not such a clumsy letter it could be called a modern.

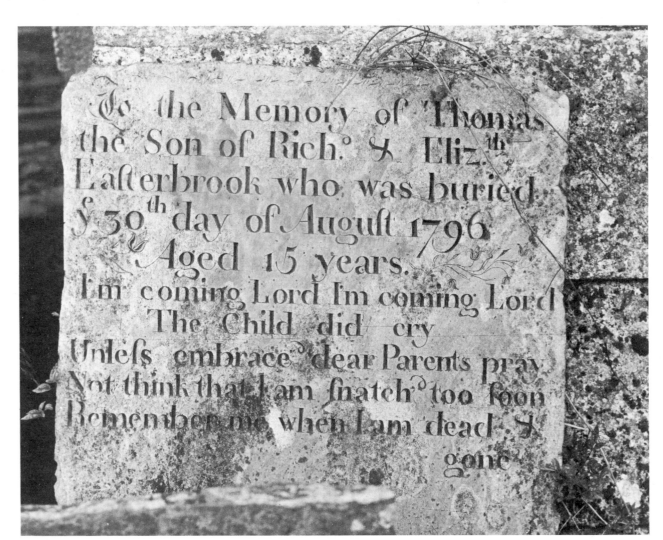

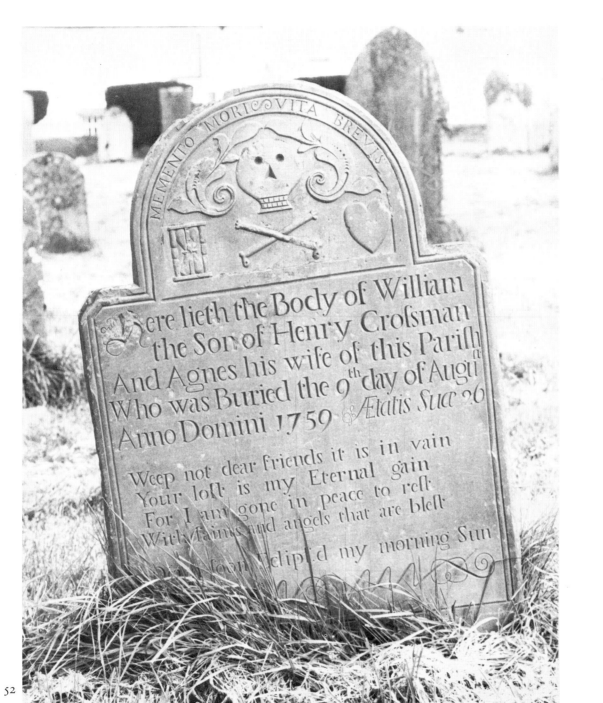

MEMENTO MORI VITA BREVIS

Here lieth the Body of William
the Son of Henry Crofsman
And Agnes his wife of this Parifh
Who was Buried the 9ᵗʰ day of Augᵘˢᵗ
Anno Domini 1759 Ætatis Suæ 26

Weep not dear friends it is in vain
Your lofs is my Eternal gain
For I am gone in peace to reft
With faints and angels that are bleft

But foon eclipt'd my morning Sun

an which was buried

it is well known

…extend
…es to…ir friend
…b…ight and true
…as th…ir due
…rougot out their day
…to re…eiue their pay
…they had serud befor
…rt for euer more
…buried in this
…tme

A memorial from Padstowe, Cornwall (**53**) – a table tomb almost buried in bushes – has a very assured and regular letterform not unlike, although better than, the previous example. The dates carved on it are 1664 and 1694: amazingly early. Presumably, like (**54**) from Egloshayle, Cornwall, dated 1721, it was cut by a supreme master lettercutter for a wealthy or aristocratic patron, while the later inferior stones we have already seen were cut by less skilled men following the tradition as best they could. Skills can decline as well as progress. If that is the case here, they picked up again, as we shall see.

Tho' now to dust her
We hope her Soul is w
But when the Sound
Raise this Same Bod
Then Shall these Bl
Receive those

scimus Enim quo
habitationis
domum non

I place this stone (55) and (56) from Callington, Cornwall, here, but it doesn't really belong. I don't know where it belongs. I have seen nothing else like it at all. I think we should just enjoy it without worrying. It has many strangely awkward features: the weights, widths and slants of the letters vary greatly and perhaps not always intentionally; the spacing is erratic; the gothic letters are oddly done; yet the overall effect has a happy, carefree sense of freedom which I wish we could regain today.

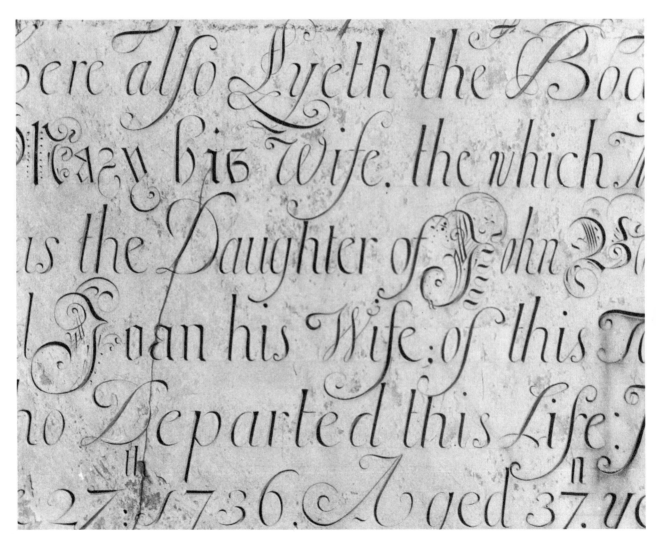

HERE Lyeth the Body
of William Ramfey; of
this Town, who departed this Life
February the 1st 1730. Aged 36 years
Here also Lyeth the Body of
Mary his Wife, the which Mary
was the Daughter of John Pomhay
and Joan his Wife, of this Town
who Departed this Life; July
the 27th 1736. Aged 37. years.
Here also Lyeth the Body of Mary
their Daughter, who Departed
this Life, April ye 17th 1733

Here Lieth the Body of
John Withycombe Who was buried
y 25ᵗʰ Day of February 1773
Aged 59 Years

In all my Life I took great pain
And ____ ways I die Refrain
____ depend
____

These two West Country stones, (57) from Tavistock and (58) from Great Torrington, both in Devon, distantly echo the previous example, and also bring us back to the somewhat similar forms we saw in Cumberland, (42) and (43). There is the same delicacy, the same restrained use of flourishes. The Torrington stone even has a similar sequence of entries, although the final one of 1829 is far less assured than the Cockermouth entry of 1797.

Although the characteristics are seen more clearly in some, all these West Country stones have shown the english letter in embryo, both in upright and in italic form.

Three monuments from **Malmesbury** Abbey, Wiltshire. The earliest (**59**) is firmly in the early English tradition. Only thirty years separate it from (**60**) and (**61**), but here a new feeling has emerged. These two are clearly by the same lettercutter who, although giving his letters angled serifs, has created a definitive english letter, with all the brilliance of a Baskerville type.

The earliest one (59) is in fact the last of the semi-naïve, semi-primitive forms we shall see in this book. From now on, all the lettering has a more knowing polish about it.

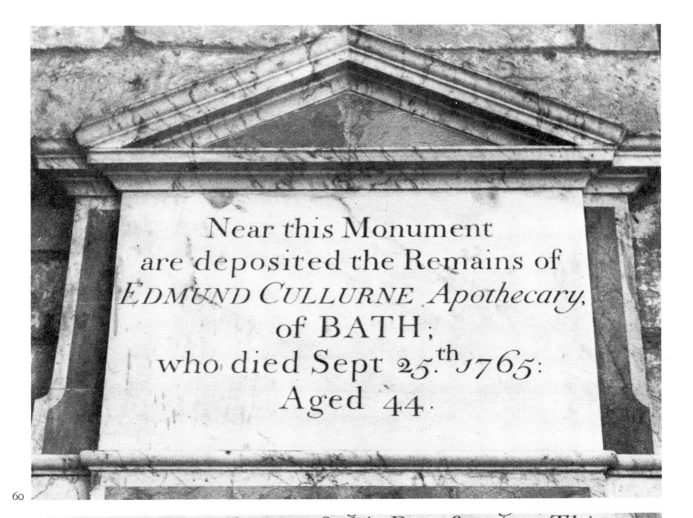

Near this Monument
are deposited the Remains of
EDMUND CULLURNE Apothecary,
of BATH;
who died Sept 25.th 1765:
Aged 44.

60

annual Distributor of this Benefaction: *Thirty
Shillings* a year to *Sarah Hughes*, his faithful Servant,
during her natural life; and after her death to be
divided in equal portions, according to the respective
Donations, above specified, to the Poor of Malmsbury,
Westport, and Burton-Hill aforesaid.

Blessed be the man who provided for the sick and needy

61

Here lieth the Body of Elizabeth the wife of Edward Coates who departed this life Septem. the 30th Anno Dom 1727 aged 39 years

Here lieth the Body of Edward Coates who departed this life on the fourth day of March Anno Dom 1728 aged 34 Years

62

We are now back around the Vale of Belvoir, and we are greeted by a dramatic change. The stones we have already seen were still being cut in 1740; but the tradition was abruptly broken as a new one took over. It was not simply different, but highly sophisticated, which certainly could not be claimed for the previous stones. The impression is given that it arrived fully developed. Strongly influenced by the writing masters, whose engraved designs could be directly translated into incised stone, the letterforms used are virtually moderns, with their sharper contrast between thicks and thins, occasionally tending towards the english letter. Free use is made of copperplate italic, and even freer use of calligrapher's flourishes. Gothic letters and other decorative letters appear, and the surrounding designs are often very complex. The style appears to be limited to the slate stones of Nottinghamshire, Leicestershire, and thereabouts.

The only intermediate stage I have noticed is a stone at Loughborough, Leicestershire (**62**), where the flourishes are more casual and the letterforms less assured than in later stones. The skills have been perfected, however, at Rempstone, Nottinghamshire (**63**). If we could use the term professional for stonecutters, we would use it here.

63

A slab at Grantham, Lincolnshire (**64**) is initialled CS; that
is, Christopher Staveley, one of the greatest of the lettercutters, who cut (11) also at Grantham. Both show total
assurance in the new style: more professionalism.

The beautiful remains seen in (65) at Loughborough sum
up the vandalism perpetuated there, where all the slabs have
been pulled up, and now lean against the graveyard banks,
or form the footpaths.

An elaborately aristocratic-looking stone can be seen in the small and remote churchyard of Granby, Nottinghamshire (66) alongside some of the early primitive stones. (67) is from Grantham.

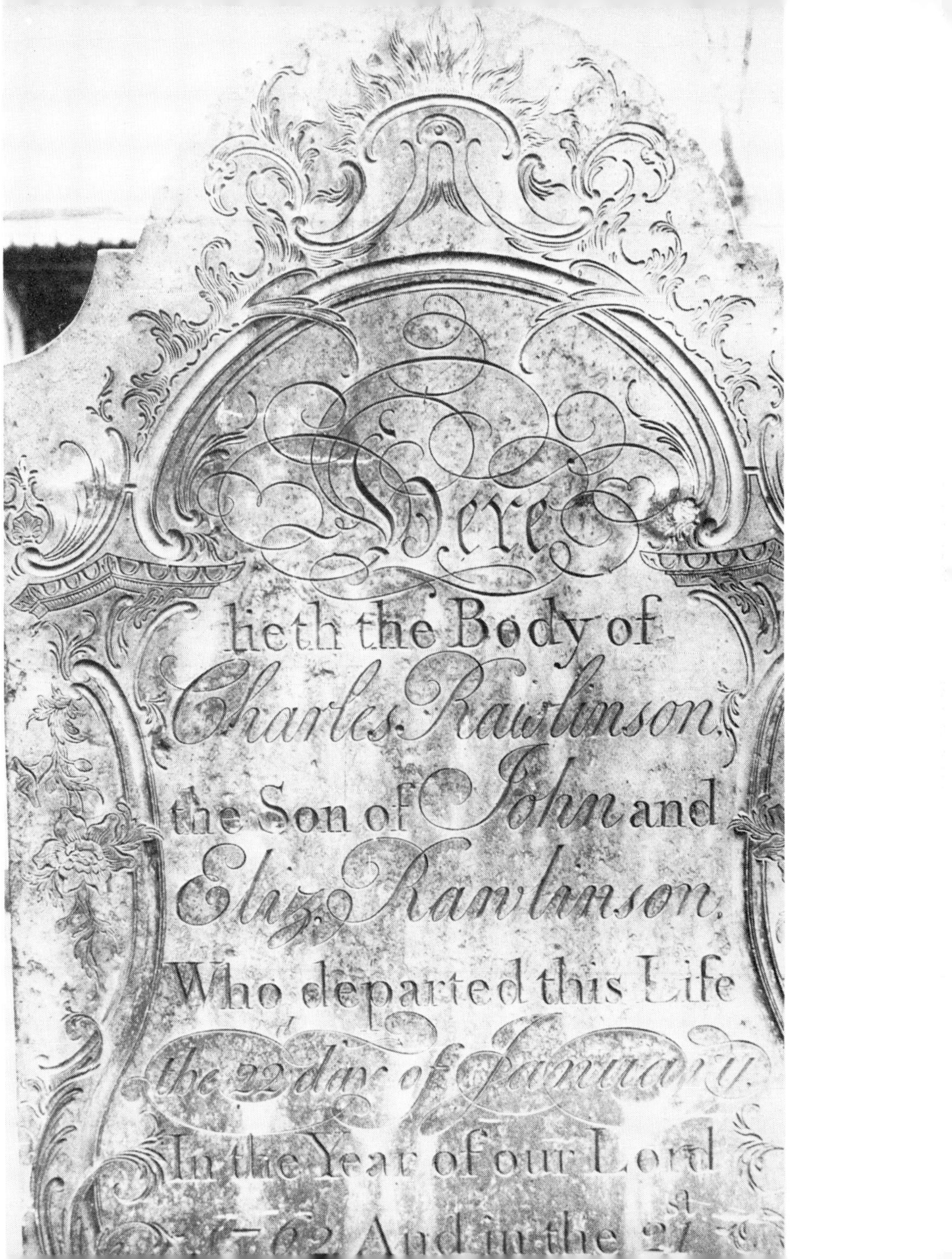

Here

lieth the Body of
Charles Rawlinson,
the Son of John and
Eliz. Rawlinson,
Who departed this Life
the 22 day of January
In the Year of our Lord

(68) with an especially rich collection of letterforms is from Long Clawson, Leicestershire; (69) is again from Granby.

In
Memory of
MARY, wife of
George Adamson
who died April 15
1797
Aged 34 Years

Dear loving, faithful...

By the end of the century, the style had declined. From Loughborough, (70) shows less discipline in its design, which is beginning to fly apart, and a more lax cutting of letters, which are wider spaced. It can be compared with (71) also from Loughborough but sixty years earlier.

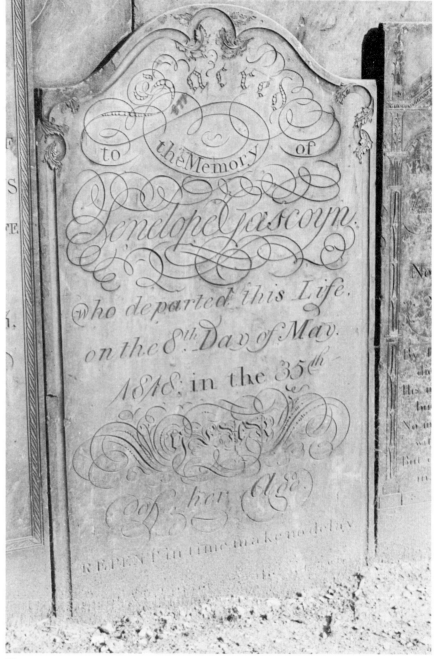

70

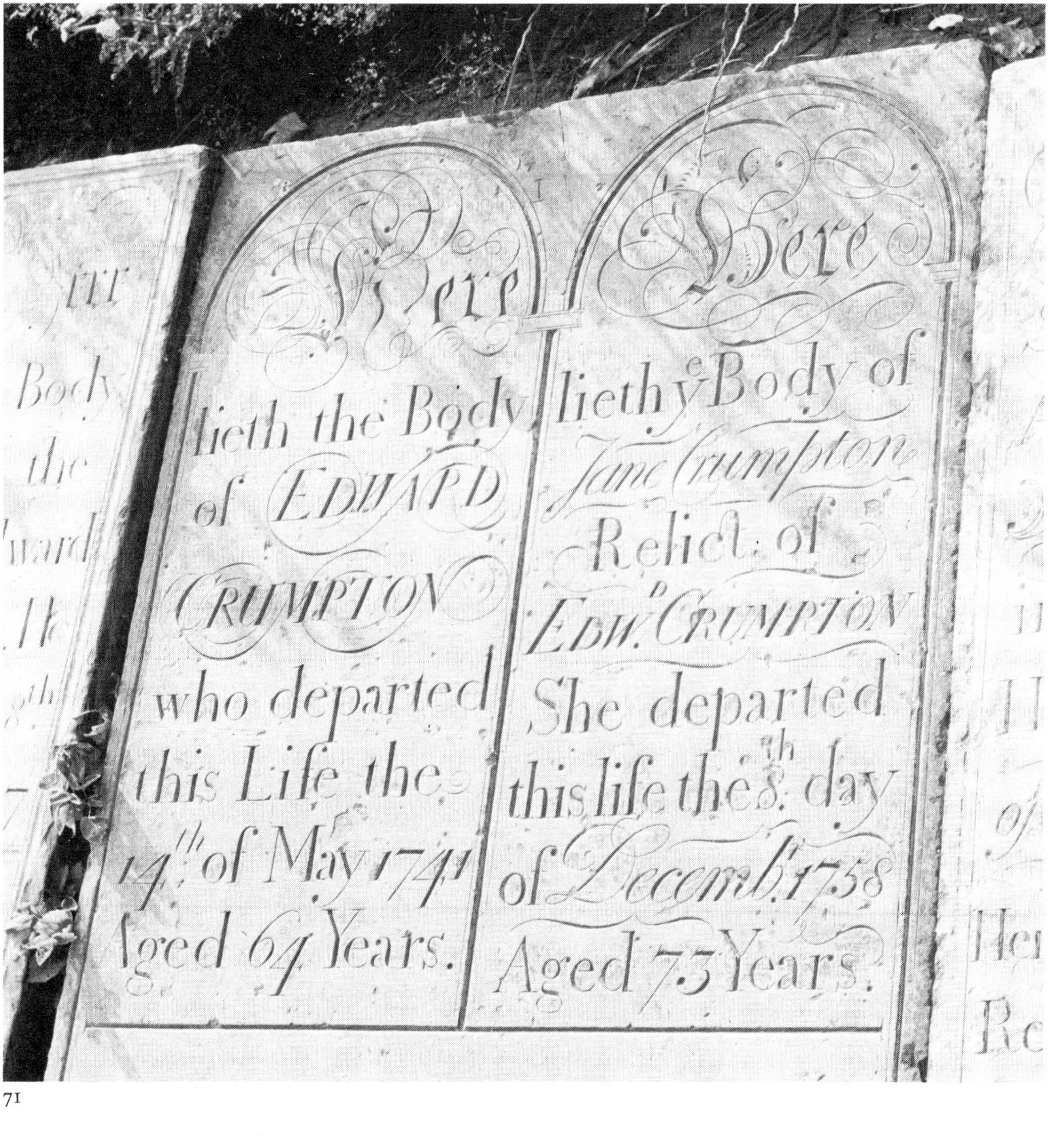
Here
lieth the Body
of EDWARD
CRUMPTON
who departed
this Life the
14th of May 1741
Aged 64 Years.
Here
lieth ye Body of
Jane Crumpton
Relict of
EDWd. CRUMPTON
She departed
this life the 8th day
of Decembr. 1758
Aged 73 Years.

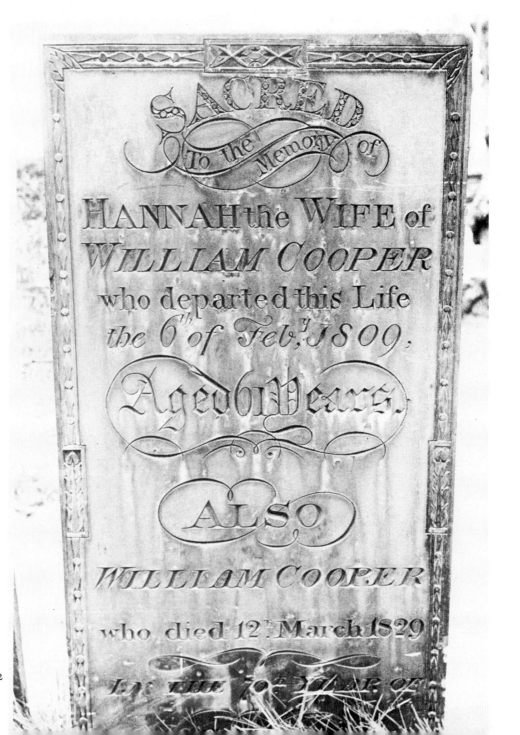

The style following the writing masters now developed into a local variant of the simpler lettercutters' tradition found elsewhere in Britain. We are about to see how this tradition developed in the North; but here at Grantham (**72**) we can see the remnants of the calligraphic style, now dead and cold. A later stone from Bottesford, Leicestershire (**73**) shows no traces of it, but has gained a new distinction. The modern has been replaced by an english letter, a less sensitive version of which can also be seen in the previous example.

Only rarely after the beginning of the nineteenth century did the Midlanders recover their old skills. In the North, as in the West Country, however, the first half of that century saw some of the best work of these regions.

This sequence from the North picks up the story we left at Cockermouth (43). A fine stone at Hebden Bridge, Yorkshire (74) shows the english letter in adolescence: full of minor eccentricities, it yet displays the characteristic plain speaking of the region.

Here resteth the Body of Robert Campbell, from Inveraray Argyle-shire North Brittain, who departed this Life the 29th day of July 1766 in the 21st Year of his Age.

695

75

In MEMORY of THOMAS BOWE, of GREAT CROSTHWAITE, Who died on the 15th of February 1838, Aged 82 years. Also of JANE his WIFE, who died on the 11th of August, 1824, aged 60 years. Also of JOHN BOWE, their Youngest Son, who died in America, June, 1825, aged 22 years.

A rather earlier stone – according to the cut date – at Burnley, Lancashire (**75**) looks considerably later, the english letter almost in its maturity. Another simple layout whose austerity has been sensitively relieved.

The definitive letterform, and style of using it, with the mixture of capitals, italic, and upright letters: Great Crosthwaite, Cumberland (**76**).

76

IN MEMORY of
Ann Daughter of Thomas and
Elizabeth Corlass of Keighley,
who died April 5th 1806,
Aged 60 Years.
ALSO of William the Son of
William and Sarah Corlass of
Bediford near Colne, who died
May 24th 1815, in the 2nd Year of
his Age.

There is nothing dry or dour about these northern stones: the english letter has a rich form, even without the occasional flourishes and decorative letters seen here at Keighley, Yorkshire (**77**). (**78**) and (**79**) from Halifax, Yorkshire, illustrate the restrained way in which the Northern cutters sometimes accepted the influence of the writing masters. The harder stone was against such *tours-de-force* as the Midlanders executed on their slate, but one feels temperament was against them too. There was certainly no lack of skill: these stones are beautifully cut in all respects.

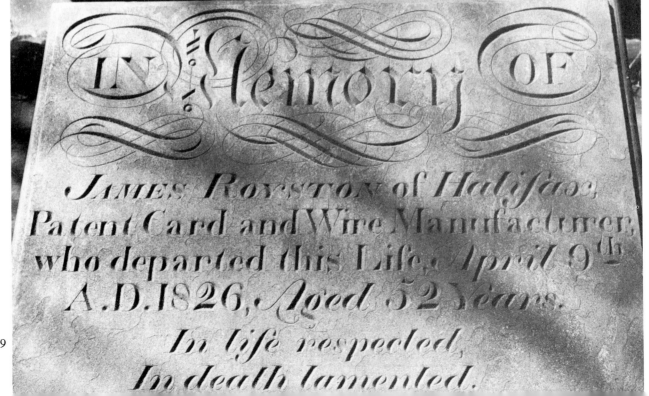

78

SARAH WILCOCK
of Halifax
died the 26th Day of July,
1803, aged forty Years.
HERE lieth also
The body of her brother
WILLIAM WILCOCK
of Halifax,

79

IN Memory OF
JAMES ROYSTON of Halifax,
Patent Card and Wire Manufacturer,
who departed this Life, April 9th
A.D. 1826, Aged 52 Years.
In life respected,
In death lamented.

This italic at Cockermouth, Cumberland (80) shows how close the form is to the signwriters' vernacular italic still to be seen on estate agents' notice boards and elsewhere. It is a lively rhythmic letter yet can be quickly cut or painted, its form deriving directly from the method of execution – either chisel or brush. This liveliness is lost in (81) from Burnley, an altogether harder and less fluent piece of cut-ting, both in the small italic and upright letters, and in the large script.

Two stones from Burnley (82) and (83) show two versions of gothic letter used for decorative effect on the first word of the inscription.

80

81

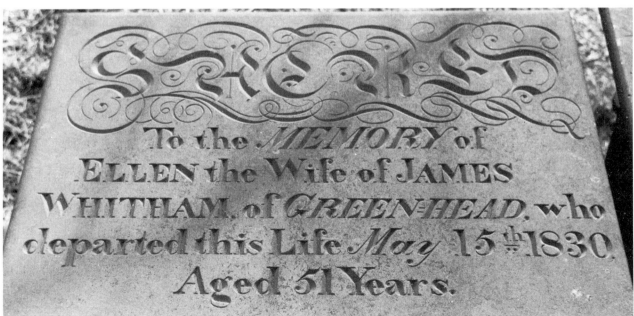

SACRED

To the MEMORY of
ALICE, the Wife of EDWARD
POLLARD of *Lower Hood House*
near *BURNLEY*, who departed this
life, *April* 22nd 1839 Aged 65 year
Also CHARLES, Son of the above

82

SACRED

To the *MEMORY* of
ELLEN the Wife of JAMES
WHITHAM, of *GREEN-HEAD*, who
departed this Life *May* 15th 1830,
Aged 51 Years.

83

Sparing use was made of the wealth of new letterforms becoming available: these two stones from Burnley, (84) and (85), use clarendons for the initial word, the second one outlined. These are the tombs of bluff, gruff, north countrymen – quite another race from namby-pamby southerners.

84

85

By the middle of the century, the designs and the letter-forms were becoming simultaneously less sensitive and less strong: drier, harder, more routine jobs, simply following, less skilfully, the old forms. Both these are from Burnley again: (86) uses an outlined clarendon and a gothic letter, (87) a gothic and a shadowed egyptian, with the main text in a humdrum grotesque.

86

87

The Northern cutters mainly followed their own lettercutting tradition. The West Country cutters, however, were influenced by the printing of the time. Although they copied the style less completely than the Midlanders copied the writing masters, they exploited the actual letterforms being invented for the industrial age. Sometimes the influence is hardly apparent, as here at Combe Martin, Devon (**88**); but a fine stone at Bodmin, Cornwall (**89**) shows fat faces (a very bold modern) mixed with italics, scripts, gothics and so on in a design reminiscent of Victorian playbills – but translated into letter-cutting terms, for the calligraphy-influenced flourishes overlapping other lines of lettering would not be possible in type.

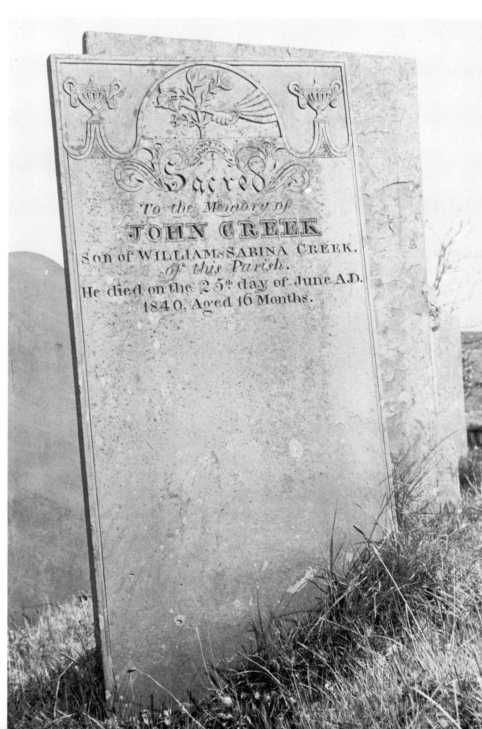

88

89

In
Memory of
JOSEPH
MERIFIELD
of S.Lawrence in this Parish who died
Novr 1 1837 Aged 14. Also of ANNE,
his daughter by Anne his wife who
June 25. 1840 Aged 15. And
of eight infant children. Likewise
of SUSANNA mother of the
above Joseph Merifield, who Died
Feby 26, 1842. Aged 75. SIMON
her husband. died at Newton in Lanivet
August 15, 1845. AGED 88.
And of Jane Merifield mother of the
above named wife of Joseph Merifield
who died July 19, 1831. Aged 75.

The Lord knoweth the days of the upright
And their inheritance shall be forever.

Two more examples show fainter echoes of the playbills: (**90**), again from Bodmin, uses a zestfully varied mixture of letterforms, with as many as five changes in one line; (**91**) from Holsworthy, Devon, generally confines these changes to the lines themselves. A good egyptian is used for the name 'Ann'.

These West Country stones have none of the simple austerity, nor the discipline, of the North; they can look thin and mean, like much Victorian bookwork. There is a suggestion of thinness in this example from Bridestowe, Devon (92), although the in-lined grotesque and waving of the name 'Martha Horn' nearly disguises it. Six different grotesques are used.

The more confident contrast of sizes and forms seen at St Teath, Cornwall (93) makes a more effective design. Here, an egyptian with a horizontal stress – another typical Victorian enrichment – and a shadowed fat face, are mingled with various forms of english letter, including an odd italic version with a horizontal stress.

IN
MEMORY
OF
SAMUEL
Son of
THOMAS H AND MARY
FAULL,
of Saint Minver:
who fell asleep in Jesus May 29,
1854,
Aged 27 Years.

SLEEP, thou art not lost, but gone before
To greet thy kindred on that happier shore
Where the tempestuous billows cease to roar

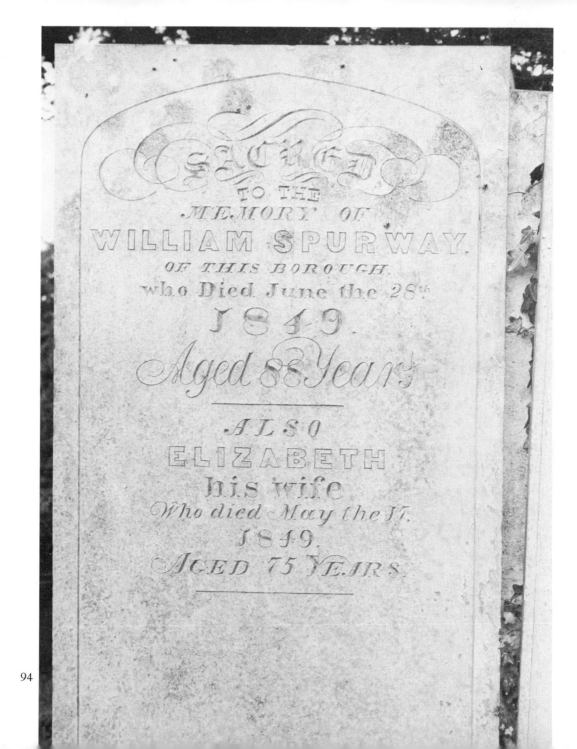

SACRED
TO THE
MEMORY OF
WILLIAM SPURWAY,
OF THIS BOROUGH,
who Died June the 28th
1849,
Aged 88 Years

ALSO
ELIZABETH
his wife
Who died May the 17,
1849,
AGED 75 YEARS.

94

A delicate, almost thin, design from Liskeard, Cornwall (**94**) has a character often to be seen in the work of Cornishmen: indescribable yet unmistakable. (**95**) from Lostwithiel, Cornwall, is less provincial in feeling, and again has been much influenced by the printing of the time.

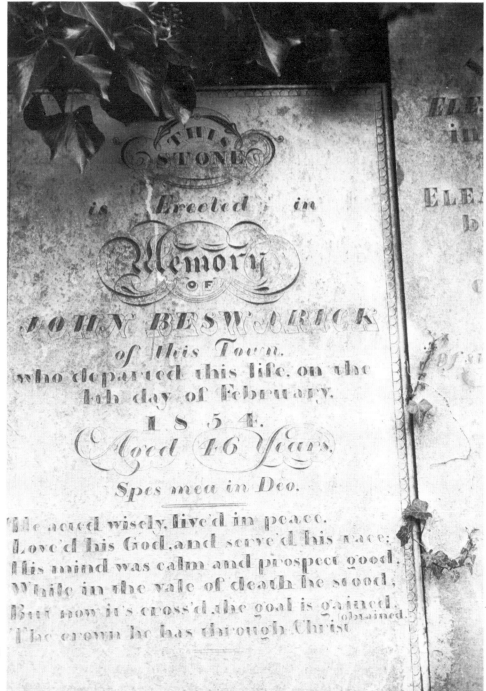

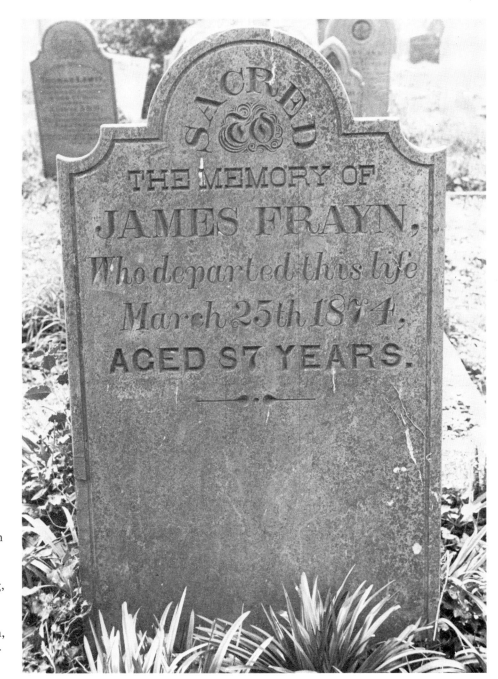

SACRED TO THE MEMORY OF JAMES FRAYN, Who departed this life March 25th 1874, AGED 87 YEARS.

(**96**) is from Egloshayle, Cornwall; (**97**) from Holsworthy, Devon, is remarkable for its boldness and simplicity – more typical of the North than the West – as well as for the late date. Most stones of this time are coldly-cut routine affairs. Such strong, rich, cutting belongs to the early 1800s. The line 'The Memory of' is cut in a horizontally-stressed egyptian, while the last line is in a grotesque un- usually good for tombstones.

Returning to Cumberland, the next eight illustrations show how the rich and varied patterns achieved with the skilful cutting of the english letter and occasional scripts degenerated to banality, false sentiment, or well-intentioned insipidity.

A fine rich stone is at Cockermouth (**98**); only slightly inferior is one at Great Crosthwaite (**99**).

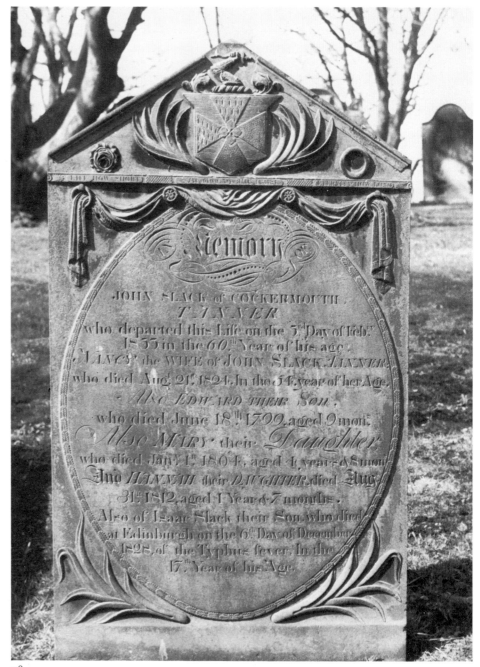

Erected IN Memory OF

TIME BRINGS ALL THINGS TO AN END.

JOSEPH CHERRY OF KESWICK: who departed this Life on the 28th Day of February 1818: in the 36th Year of *his age.*

Also of MARY the *Daugr* of Josr & Elizr Cherry *Who* died on the 28r of September 1817 aged 9 years & 6 Mor.

Also of ANN their Daughter who died on the 9th of March 1815, aged 1 Year & 5 Mons.

Also of JOHN their SON who died on the 21r of Febry 1817 aged 1 Year & 7 Mon.

Also of ELIZABETH their Daughter who died on the 24th Day of March 1819 aged 1 Year & 4 Mons.

ALSO of *Joseph Hudson* of THE Royal Oak Hotel, Keswick, who departed this Life on the 14th of Decr 1855, In the 59th *Year* of his Age.

ALSO of MARGARET his *Wife,* who died at KESWICK: and was interred at *Ambleside,* in the *Parish* of Grasmere on the 11r of *Sep.r* 1828, In the 28th *Year* of her Age.

ALSO OF ELIZABETH RELICT OF THE ABOVE JOSEPH HUDSON, AND WIDOW OF THE above NAMED JOSEPH CHERRY, WHO DEPARTED THIS LIFE ON THE 5th Day of Decr 1855, in the 71r Year of her Age.

The decline of a splendid tradition. But these Great Crosthwaite stones are better than most of this period, perhaps because of the isolation of Cumberland, aided by the ready availability of slate. The italic on (**100**) still has some life to it, while the english capitals on (**101**) are still decent, if a little drily done.

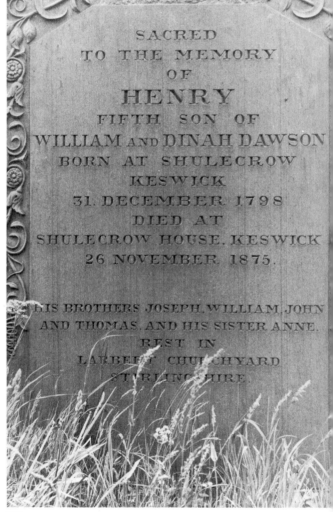

Odd things happened later. With the loss of confidence in a style of their own period, both arts and crafts plundered the past. Celtic crosses and primitive letterforms reappeared. (**102**) and (**103**) are again from Great Crosthwaite, and both, in their lettering, look back to examples such as (6), although using a more regular, and more knowing, letterform.

102

103

To this sad state has the craft descended – and far worse. At least these two, (**104**) and (**105**), again from Great Crosthwaite, are cut in pleasing irregular lumps of sympathetic and unpolished stone; but letterforms and layout are mundane.

104

105

A rather different kind of lettercutter from those whose work forms the bulk of this book is self-conscious craftsman following the tradition of the Arts and Crafts Movement. One of the best of its kind that I have seen – they are not common – is this stone from Bibury, Gloucestershire (106) by Simon Verity. Here is an attempt to create something more original, showing a love of and a feeling for letterforms. Perhaps it is just a *little* self-conscious; but how much better than the style of almost all the stones done today, of which I cannot bring myself to show even one.

A small unpretentious group of stones at Carbury, Co. Leix, are the only ones I have seen which appear to have been cut in the unselfconscious way of the great tradition. This example (**107**) shows the kind of letterform used – an original grotesque revealing that the cutter is aware of what is happening elsewhere, but which has not been copied from any particular form.

More self-aware – yet less so, to my eyes, than the stone at Bibury (106) – is this wood slab at Wadhurst, Sussex (**108**). Cut in relief in a simple sans serif, it faintly recalls some of the very early primitive stones with its tight block of closely spaced lines.

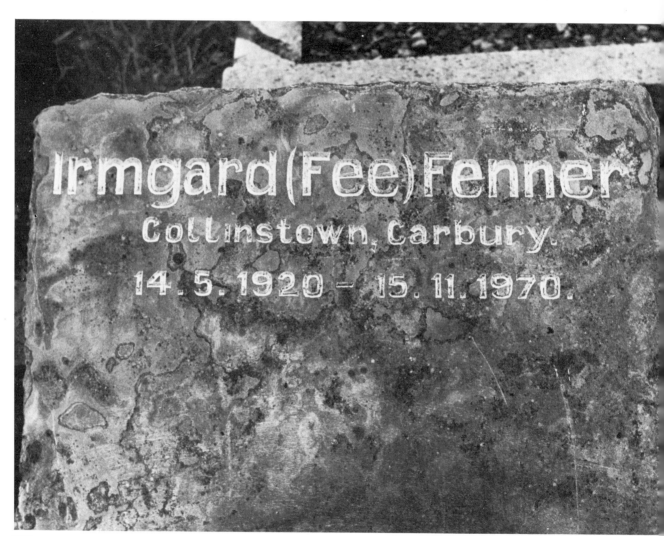

If, when hearing that I have been stilled at last, they stand at the door,
  Watching the full-starred heavens that winter sees,
Will this thought rise on those who will meet my face no more,
  'He was one who had an eye for such mysteries'?

And will any say when my bell of quittance is heard in the gloom,
  And a crossing breeze cuts a pause in its outrollings,
Till they rise again, as they were a new bell's boom,
  'He hears it not now, but used to notice such things'?

Hardy was glumly asking that in 1917, towards the end of
his long life. Sixty years later, we can be even more doubt-
ing that we will be much remembered. 'We are too menny',
and our expectation of life is twice that of many whose
tombs we have seen in this book. So many lives, and so
many deaths; who cares? Perhaps only when the dead are
young will much be made of death; as here, rather
movingly, at Wadhurst, (**109**) and (**110**).

But if the carving of memorials to dead men is generally a decayed and unwanted craft, the same skills could be revived for other purposes. From *The Observer* for 8 May 1977:

'Odd things happen in the parks. In Kensington Gardens, someone has suddenly erected a mysterious spiralling stone, marking the place where there used to be a spring, which has now dried up. Whose idea was it suddenly to commemorate a dried-up spring, an historical item of no conceivable interest to anyone?'

Blind springs were the centres of early religions, theoretically and practically. Primary geodetic lines, dowsers observe, always take a spiral form at such places. While this stone, (**111**) and (**112**), which serves as a drinking fountain, is a little lumpen and lacking in grace – and the lettering rather traditional – its design has been governed by the spiral, the inscription winding around five and a half times.

The general thesis of Michael Davie's article, quoted above, is 'Must public sculpture be so awful?' We are in full agreement with him there. But does he believe the source of water to be really of no interest to man today? Precisely because we no longer have an eye for such mysteries – our archetypal instincts regarding nature being overlaid with the trappings of other religions – we need to be reminded of them.

111

112

There is an increasing general interest in the attitudes of early man, no matter how much archaeologists may bristle at talk of earth currents and alignments. Fallacies they may be, or may not be, but only good can result from anything which helps to reawaken our awareness of natural forces. Man has become too big for his boots; he cannot ignore nature with impunity, and it is good for him to be reminded of this.

Memorials to springs – whether dried-up or not – and similar natural phenomena revered by early man, or reminders of nature (such as streams now underground) within intensely urban areas, could have an important part to play in our imaginative life. They could be memorials which not only tell us of things past, but which enhance our appreciation of the present. A form of poetry. So they should be conceived in a creative way. Lettering, or lettered sculpture, treated with contemporary feeling, would be a much more acceptable form of public sculpture than most recent work, and could be a source of interest in itself as well as a source of information.

Besides reminding us of our natural roots, memorials can show us our historical roots. We have in Britain hundreds, perhaps thousands, of plaques or notices indicating historical buildings, historical events, birthplaces of writers, and the like. Rarely is the lettering more than decent, rarely worthy of its subject. Our present pervasive nostalgia, an uncreative emotion, could be turned to creative ends. These plaques and notices, which are read with quite extraordinary fascination by the general public, should also become a source of visual as well as factual interest. People actually visit graveyards, after all, merely to look at the old lettering and read the inscriptions. A harmless pleasure, and a small one. Life is made of trivialities.

If we ignore our roots, natural and historical, we impoverish and diminish ourselves. We become two-dimensional.

For, wonning in these ancient lands,
Enchased and lettered as a tomb,
And scored with prints of perished hands,
And chronicled with dates of doom,
Though my own Being bear no bloom,
I trace the lives such scenes enshrine,
Give past examplars present room,
And their experience count as mine.   Hardy